Komodo Dragons

by Megan Borgert-Spaniol

BELLWETHER MEDIA • MINNEAPOLIS, MN

Note to Librarians, Teachers, and Parents:

Blastoff! Readers are carefully developed by literacy experts and combine standards-based content with developmentally appropriate text.

Level 1 provides the most support through repetition of high-frequency words, light text, predictable sentence patterns, and strong visual support.

Level 2 offers early readers a bit more challenge through varied simple sentences, increased text load, and less repetition of high-frequency words.

Level 3 advances early-fluent readers toward fluency through increased text and concept load, less reliance on visuals, longer sentences, and more literary language.

Level 4 builds reading stamina by providing more text per page, increased use of punctuation, greater variation in sentence patterns, and increasingly challenging vocabulary.

Level 5 encourages children to move from "learning to read" to "reading to learn" by providing even more text, varied writing styles, and less familiar topics.

Whichever book is right for your reader, Blastoff! Readers are the perfect books to build confidence and encourage a love of reading that will last a lifetime!

This edition first published in 2014 by Bellwether Media, Inc.

No part of this publication may be reproduced in whole or in part without written permission of the publisher. For information regarding permission, write to Bellwether Media, Inc., Attention: Permissions Department, 5357 Penn Avenue South, Minneapolis, MN 55419.

Library of Congress Cataloging-in-Publication Data

Borgert-Spaniol, Megan, 1989- author.
  Komodo Dragons / by Megan Borgert-Spaniol.
    pages cm. – (Blastoff! Readers. Animal Safari)
  Summary: "Developed by literacy experts for students in kindergarten through grade three, this book introduces Komodo dragons to young readers through leveled text and related photos"– Provided by publisher.
  Audience: 5 to 8.
  Audience: K to grade 3.
  Includes bibliographical references and index.
  ISBN 978-1-60014-967-2 (hardcover : alk. paper)
  1. Komodo dragon–Juvenile literature. I. Title. II. Series: Blastoff! readers. 1, Animal safari.
  QL666.L29B67 2014
  597.95'968–dc23
                                                                                              2014000108

Printed in the United States of America, North Mankato, MN.

Contents

What Are Komodo Dragons?

Komodo dragons are the largest lizards on Earth.

They live in warm forests and **savannahs**.

Finding Food

Komodo dragons are **scavengers**. They use their tongues to smell for food.

They also hunt
deer, wild pigs,
and other animals.
Some eat young
Komodo dragons.

A Komodo dragon bites with sharp teeth. Its **venom** kills the **prey**.

Komodo dragons share a kill. They eat chunks of meat whole.

Males, Females, and Babies

Male Komodo dragons fight for females. They stand on their back legs and **wrestle**.

Females lay 15 to 30 eggs. Babies **hatch** from the eggs.

The young live in
trees. Adults cannot
eat them there.
Stay safe,
little dragon!

Glossary

hatch—to break out of a shell

prey—animals that are hunted by other animals for food

savannahs—grasslands with scattered trees

scavengers—animals that feed on the meat of dead animals

venom—liquid that can kill an animal or make it unable to move

wrestle—to fight by holding and pushing

To Learn More

AT THE LIBRARY

Marsh, Laura F. *Lizards*. Washington, D.C.: National Geographic Society, 2012.

Marsico, Katie. *A Komodo Dragon Hatchling Grows Up*. New York, N.Y.: Children's Press, 2007.

Rudolph, Jessica. *My Claws Are Large and Curved*. New York, N.Y.: Bearport Publishing, 2014.

ON THE WEB

Learning more about Komodo dragons is as easy as 1, 2, 3.

1. Go to www.factsurfer.com.

2. Enter "Komodo dragons" into the search box.

3. Click the "Surf" button and you will see a list of related web sites.

With factsurfer.com, finding more information is just a click away.

Index